THE LITTLE VOICES OF THE PEARS

THE

LITTLE

VOICES

OF THE

PEARS

HERBERT MORRIS

PERENNIAL LIBRARY

HARPER & ROW, PUBLISHERS, New York
Grand Rapids, Philadelphia, St. Louis, San Francisco
London, Singapore, Sydney, Tokyo

The following poems originally appeared elsewhere: "The Wait" in *Pequod*; "Latin" and "French" in *Poetry*; "Reading to the Children" and "Lincoln's Hat" in *The Hudson Review*; "William James in Brazil" in *The New Criterion*; "Olana, Summer, 1872" in *The Massachusetts Review*.

FIRST EDITION

Designed by Karen Savary

Library of Congress Cataloging-in-Publication Data

Morris, Herbert, 1928–
    The little voices of the pears/Herbert Morris. —1st ed.
        p.   cm.
    Poems.
    ISBN 0-06-055163-1
    ISBN 0-06-096363-8 (pbk.)
    I. Title.
PS3563.O87434L5   1989   88-45951
811'.54—dc19

---

89 90 91 92 93 DT/HC 10 9 8 7 6 5 4 3 2 1
89 90 91 92 93 DT/HC 10 9 8 7 6 5 4 3 2 1 (pbk.)

For Ashley Baquero

And what more need be said of it than this?

CONTENTS

THE LITTLE VOICES OF THE PEARS

THE WAIT

Russell Lee, "Saturday Afternoon Street Scene"
Welch, McDowell County, West Virginia, August 24, 1946

Looking at it long enough, looking at it
not for the first time or the last, one feels
wave after wave of something coming down,
strangeness, displacement, utter desolation—
part heat, yes, part humidity, but mostly
some pure, unnamed, late August suffocation:
life in small towns on main streets some time after
the peace treaties have been signed, the surrenders,
with all the ceremony one expects,
or might expect, witnessed, proclaimed, accepted,
trees motionless, if there are trees, air still,
dense clouds, should there be clouds, lowering, lowered,
the date 1946, though the date
could be anytime after war, before,
even, given the proper climate, during
(history need not enter here, the great
tidal sweep of events played out in public,
its stages vast, far-flung, need not intrude),
the place called West Virginia, though it could be
east, north, or south, as well, all places, none,
that place wholly without place, placeless, nameless
(the cartographer's art is wholly lost here,
wholly obsolete, wholly unavailing).

*

In letters two or three feet tall, letters
with which one might, in time, with care, great care,
a care so infinite one cannot weigh it,
piece together, attempt to piece together,
an alphabet, a word, the very music
working its way beneath what we call language,
letters a man perched on a ladder takes down
each Saturday, past midnight, in their place
hoisting next week's star, next week's feature, Van Johnson
looms from the marquee of the Pocahontas,
BORN FOR TROUBLE spelled out beneath his name,
rimmed by small light bulbs blinking on and off
(it will be hours until the dark falls here),
though one remains in doubt whether it might be
June Allyson or Gloria de Haven
Van spends eight reels in wry, smiling pursuit of
five times a day, six times on Saturday
(either will do, and do quite handsomely),
plot unchanging, dialogue locked in, holding,
tomorrow spinning out, spun out, in place,
unaltered and unalterable, fixed,
before one knows what one might do or say,
before one laughs, breaks into tears, does nothing,
before the players can cry Wait, or Stop,
unwind the reel, reorchestrate the future,
begin (if it were possible) again.

Traffic, this afternoon, moves slowly: roadsters
jam the three-block main street now, strollers walk
in groups, some two-by-two, pass on the sidewalks
flanking the street. Platoons of parking meters
stand at attention, single file, on both curbs,
near side, far side, and a portion of sky,
partial, pinched-off, less than a sky, reluctant
even to be included, it would seem,

ungenerous, unyielding, swept with omens,
can be glimpsed in the background, raw, unclear,
a sky from which, all day, something is falling,
gray, off-gray, a sky drained of everything
but the burden of rain it carries, rain
always impending, never coming down.
At the end of this main street, two or three blocks
from where we are positioned, a small mountain,
foliage seen in silhouette, blurred, hazy,
where mountain turns to sky, or sky to mountain,
asserts itself, almost precipitously,
its angle of ascent, the suddenness
with which it rises, towers, looms, the awesome
quality of its darkness, volume, shape,
intractable, mysterious, perverse,
threatening, even, somehow fraught with danger.

Equally dangerous (or, in time, more so)
may be the fresh, white shirt of the man lounging
in the company of two women, two
young West Virginia women, at the shoe store,
women who, it appears, have been to shop,
holding, each of them, small store bags before them,
emblems of what they did, of where they went,
of what may have detained them on their way here.
The man is holding nothing, has not shopped,
has not even made plans, perhaps, to shop,
may have little heart for it, possibly
has decided to put it off for next time,
should there be a next time, for the time after,
even to put it off indefinitely,
knows there is nothing that he needs now, nothing,
nothing he can buy, nothing that he wants
worth the stupendous effort, as he sees it,
to shop, to be a shopper (and for what?),

street by street, store by store, window by window,
to look, to price, compare, admire, look once more,
go back, make certain, look, look again, want,
that, perhaps, more than anything: to want;
nothing he wants to want, as he might phrase it,
should he have found the will, the words, to phrase it,
nothing he wants to want again, no, nothing,
nothing he wants to have he does not have,
nothing he wants to need more than he needs,
not the shoes in the window (his may last
as long as shoes last, which is time enough:
as for "fashion," he may not know what that is),
not even a new summer shirt (his shirt
will, he thinks, take him where he needs to go,
where he feels he must go now, even further),
darkness falling, but not yet fallen, rain
threatening to come down, not coming down,
heat, humidity, mountain, sky, late summer
of 1946, whenever that was,
whatever one feels, may have felt, could not feel,
whatever one thinks, or shall think, one can read
into another's life, or time, or fate,
as he leans at the window of the shoe store
in the company of two women, waiting
(waiting as though there were no end to waiting),
and however mistaken or unerring
one's insights into what was said, was not said,
may have been said, that summer afternoon,
these women to this man, or he to them,
air from the Pocahontas dark and cool
as it spills from the lobby to the street,
street by street, store by store, window by window,
Van Johnson BORN FOR TROUBLE, as the sign reads,
June or Gloria knowing no reprieve,
no relief, from the loveliest bombardment

a girl at MGM might need or want,
Van prodigious in those attempts to charm:
those eyes, those teeth, those grins, those absolutes
of lilacs-by-back-fences, optimism,
cottage curtains of blue-and-white checked muslin,
happiness (being happy, staying happy),
what one might lie awake, nights, dreaming of
in 1946, plotting, composing,
believing in, believing in: the future.

He leans against the window, leans and waits,
that already illuminated window
(though it is afternoon, some fair, far distance,
one knows, from here to darkness) of the shoe store,
behind him a five-tiered display case sporting
the latest in men's stylings (wingtips, brogues),
level heaped on level, pyramid-fashion,
arranged with care, meticulously, each pair
peering into the street at the same angle,
not, pair to pair, the slightest deviation,
with not the merest whisper of disruption
to flood their soles, to stain them, happy shoes,
tips polished, gleaming, catching what one might call
light under more auspicious circumstances,
their voices meager, frail, their song thin, too.
The women stand relaxed, seem to be fixed
(might "caught" have done their straits the greater justice?)
at the brink of decision, some dim juncture
where past and future coalesce, but not quite,
between determinations, one might call it,
their location not here and yet not there,
indeterminate for the present,·which,
from the evidence, all one dare intuit
from this distance, seems not to present them,
either of them, with undue difficulty.

They wait, they are content to wait; if waiting
is the thing they are called on here to do,
waiting the name of the thing they must pass through,
if the wait proves, at best, brief, temporary,
should it be, seem to be, for reasons never
fully nor satisfactorily rendered,
what one does on a street in West Virginia
some late Saturday afternoon, a summer
after a war, before, it shall not matter,
Van Johnson, next door, finely freckled, courting
June Allyson or Gloria de Haven,
there seems little to do, then, but to wait,
to do no more nor less than what they do,
with whatever serenity or grace
one is able, may be able, to muster
two or three nondescript blocks of a main street
from, on one side, a mountain, haze-wreathed, rising,
rising ominously, precipitously,
and, on the other, a late August sky,
all gray, dull gray, slate gray, unrelieved, choked,
a sky at once too close, too far, all day
promising (or is the word threatening?)
to release what it cannot quite release.

Though they may have arrived together, these three,
one comes to feel the man is waiting longer,
that, whatever they wait for (look, now: notice
how the others, this August afternoon,
amble, walk the street, pause at intersections
until a crossing seems convenient. These three,
two young women, a man in a white shirt,
linger, loiter, listen perhaps for thunder,
though rain has not yet fallen, shall not fall,
seem to have little to do now but wait,
nowhere to go, no appointments to keep,

nothing, apart from this, to occupy them,
to hold them, somehow root them, in time save them),
his wait alone will not be temporary,
his alone will not soon be terminated.
One thinks, all the while, of their gift for patience,
thinks of restraint, enduring, limitless,
the quietness of all they do and are,
is persuaded to think even of passion,
even of passion, in such bleak, cramped streets,
that curve of wrist, thigh, ankle, luminescent
even in this obscure light, even in
some West Virginia of the mind, far inland,
farther than far, darkness falling, late daylight
settling on them, things coming down, something
(unnamed, unnameable) advancing on them
(sky? mountain? cloak of darkness? rain? loss? anguish?),
time passed, time passing, or about to pass
(appointments never kept, or never made,
promises given those one loved, could not love,
loved insufficiently, perhaps loved too much),
their faces clear, their eyes calm (more than clear,
more than calm), what one takes for clear, for calm,
their composure at once ambiguous,
exemplary, informed by some pale splendor
one admits somehow to having foreclosed,
abandoned hope for here, as with much else,
given the unknowns of the situation,
the imponderables called West Virginia,
the sense, no less pervasive for its vagueness,
of an abyss impending, of abysses,
the unfathomability (black roadsters
making progress, barely, in traffic, Van
persistent at the back fence, under lilac,
buoyant, resilient, in long-running courtship—
five times daily, six today, Saturday—

of June (blonde bangs) or Gloria (blonde ringlets),
strollers knowing where to go, seeming to know
where to go, crossing, soon to cross, not crossing,
where their steps might be taking them, each holding,
holding firmly, as firmly as the mind holds,
to one idea, one, just one, each sensing—
the exactness of it, the fine precision,
perfect in its dimensions, shapely, thrilling—
mission, purpose, above all destination)
of how long they must wait, of what to wait for.

The man holds nothing, as has been reported;
he leans against the plate-glass of the shoe store,
his summer shirt given back in reflection,
right arm hanging against his side, the other
casually thrust in a trouser pocket,
both shirt cuffs rolled neatly above the wrists.
Five tiers of wingtips, brogues, gleam fiercely, fiercely
(order, thy name is wingtips; speak of chaos
softly here, should you speak of it at all);
all day weather has fallen, all day, all day,
dull gray, off-gray, slate gray, continues falling.
For the moment he is expressionless,
if not content to wait, perhaps resigned
to the knowledge that what he does he must do,
must do here, in this place, that what he suffers
shall not be the first or last of it somehow,
that, however long the women have waited,
he is waiting longer, much longer, longer
than whatever waiting one can envision,
hopes to envision, that, in fact, his fate,
can he be said to have a fate, is that,
just that, precisely that, no more than that:
to wait, at the end of waiting to wait

again, or further, or, this time, more darkly,
more profoundly, difficultly, immensely.

The shirt the man wears (here the ground shifts, slippage
begins, persists, intensifies, a downward
slide, a falling upward, a dislocation
impossible to overstate the depth of,
consonant with whatever came before,
though nothing can be said to have prepared us,
to have assured our certainty, our footing)
will be for one to do with as one can.
I cannot tell you what shall be made of it,
this intrusion of white, this field of blindness,
the thing that one goes back to and goes back to
as though it held some secret, as it may,
even the glimmer which the shoe store window
where we glimpse them waiting (the symmetry
of brogues and wingtips stunningly aligned
in five ascending tiers of a display case
intact, intact, unimpaired, anchoring us
with an inexplicable poignancy
to a semblance of order, of control,
in a landscape stricken with incongruence),
seems, with an inadvertence not quite random,
to have mirrored exactly, to have snared.
It may well have to do (my footing here
falters, grows treacherous, seems nonexistent)
with what threatens to fall at any moment,
fall hard, on what we have agreed to call,
by prearrangement whose specific terms
have not been revealed to us, West Virginia,
those imponderables called West Virginia,
Saturday, late August, after a war
half-forgotten—or is it half-remembered?—

(we are standing at a distance equal
to one or to the other, some vague mid-point
where names dim, battles blur, causes seem garbled:
forgive us our forgetfulness, our losses);
with a mountain whose talent it shall be
to inch closer the farther it recedes
into a background indistinguishable
from foreground, should the terminology,
the word, the alphabet, the very music,
any longer matter this afternoon,
too late, too dim, too distant, much too long
after the war, the treaties, the surrenders,
the half-remembering, the half-forgetting,
whatever trouble Van may have been born for,
whatever trouble each of us is born for,
so far from the sea they must be, so far,
so long without music they seem, so long
the dry spell, dreamlessness, so fierce the man's shirt,
dazzle, blindness, the color waiting must be.

LATIN

We are, once more, in Mrs. Goodman's class,
geraniums crowding the sun-struck windows.
I occupy the third desk, second row,
on which are carved initials of those students

who grappled here with Latin long before me.
An inkwell has been drilled into the wood,
upper right, and the slender legs, cast iron,
filigree grillwork, grip the creaking floor.

I wear those trousers woven of rough tweed,
their color some drab brown the shade of mud.
Mrs. Goodman wears one of her black wigs,
hair black as night, each styled in the same fashion,

bangs fringing the pale forehead, two spit curls
glued to the temples, cut to slash each cheek.
She paces back and forth, tapping a pointer
against the blackboard with each definition,

predicate, object, subject, gerund, noun,
seven uses of the conditional,
one more subtle than the next, more exotic,
"should she," "were I," "could you," "if we," "might someone."

Some days she smells of lilac, some days jasmine.
She wears black fishnet stockings, kidskin pumps
with thin spike heels four inches high; her hemline
grazes a calf as shapely as her ankles.

Today, it seems, we come to the subjunctive,
but we approach it sideways, from behind,
advance on it as if by inadvertence,
almost refrain from mentioning its name

(a backward look, a sideways look, a glance,
less than a glance, a glimpse, with eyes half-closed),
slowly, quietly, with great stealth, great care,
that care beyond mere care, are made to sense

an assault broader, bolder, more head-on,
an advance other than by indirection,
might very well, students, frighten it off.
I am twelve that winter, perhaps thirteen.

I love this room; love the geraniums
misting the panes, pane by pane, with their breath,
reaching in one direction for the sun;
love the fragrance of ink the monitor

pours at each desk from a tall, capped blue bottle,
the spout held low, just so, that it not leak;
love the feel of the tweed scraping my legs
when I stir in my seat or rise to speak.

Impatience rides the morning, restlessness
half the afternoon: I want time to pass
until we climb the dim flight to 310.
The bell rings; clamor; scuffle; we change rooms.

At two-fifteen, precisely, we begin
(the sun cuts diamonds on the frosted panes),
predicate, object, subject, gerund, noun,
stand, one by one, when called on, read from Caesar

(battle on wind-swept plains, snow in high passes),
translations knotted, tangled, rock-strewn, dense
(now the strategic pause, the cough, the stutter),
pored over, worked, reworked, pulled this way, that,

to fit our stumbling, to accommodate
the desperation seizing us mid-plot,
hesitation a tense unto itself
having to do with ignorance, not grammar.

(That winter was the winter syntax seemed
a route to all I thought I wished to be,
who I wished to become, the agent by which
one was delivered, somewhere, to one's self,

the magic which, in time, bestows, transforms,
that, if one could piece the sentence together,
word by word, step by step, worked and reworked,
if one might learn the phrasing, deep and clear,

as clear as water, say, as deep as night,
it might well lead, or open, to one's life;
if one could learn the principle involved,
one might know how to live, or what to live for.)

I love the scent wild lilac trails, or jasmine,
as she patrols the aisles between the desks
attending to the pains of conjugation,
reminding us verbs shall agree with subjects;

love to move my fingers across the grain,
touching the nicks and grooves of old initials,
the cold, forged latticework of iron legs
swirling gracefully, looping to the floor;

love even the chipped song the radiator
rouses itself to sing these afternoons,
plaintive, tentative, frail, occasionally
wavering, in a voice reedy and thin.

I am twelve, as I said, perhaps thirteen,
sit in the sun, diamonds etched on my lids,
grapple with Latin each day at my desk
(not yet having carved my HM across it,

never having carved my HM across it),
predicate, object, subject, gerund, noun,
rising to read, when called on, hesitation,
as always, trailing me, my twin, my double,

student of light, of language, of that longing
rooted in neither, yet rooted in both,
finding my way, losing my way, those passes
profound, immense, endlessly taxing, all but

impenetrable, untranslatable,
should she, were I, could you, if we, might someone,
having waited all day for afternoon,
for this moment, yet dreading being called on,

content, for now, to wait for light to pour
(light pours, light pours), for gifts to be bestowed
(gifts, that winter, are not to be bestowed),
comprehension, fluency, grace, sheer daring,

all that might matter most to Mrs. Goodman,
all that might matter most, that year, to me,
for the radiator to sing its song
and the sun to cut diamond after diamond

afternoons on the frost-encrusted panes;
for, best of all, Mrs. Goodman to enter
at two-fifteen, precisely, to begin
(her stride high-arched, deliberate, seamless, slow),

the plains wind-swept, the passes lashed with snow.
I read, read poorly; Mrs. Goodman points
to her head, her black-banged, black spit-curled head,
cries "Lapsa de memoria," cries it twice.

I pause, I cough, I stutter, start to blush
("Lapsa de memoria"), yet persist.
Mrs. Goodman moves to my side, corrects me
(waves of lilac and jasmine overwhelm me,

I, who fail, for some reason, to remember
the deepest needs of the infinitive,
exchange pronoun for noun, invert the order
by which all parts—the world, as well?—cohere),

asking what one is to do with the clause
it seems one quite forgot, the participle
one decimated, dropped, wanting to know
how one is to live, what one is to live for.

READING TO THE CHILDREN

The first child asks me: Are these poems yours?
The second asks: Where do you get ideas?
The third child says: I have always loved poems.
The fourth child wonders: What makes poems poems?
The fifth one asks: Which of them is your favorite?
The sixth one asks me: Is there ice cream later?
The seventh child asks: Is a poem dreaming?

To the first, who now fidgets with her hair,
inspects her nails, her dress, who may, in fact,
have little need to know what she has asked,
for whom the question, as well as the answer,
may well prove merely one more temporary
distraction in a day filled with distractions,
I say: Yes, these are poems I have written.
I could read no one else's half so clearly,
with as much feeling, as I read you these;
that, more than anything, may be what I would
leave with you, feeling—music, of course, meaning,
certainly, but first feeling, feeling foremost.

The second child, holding his head to one side
as he speaks, pokes a finger in his ear,
looks at me as a child looks at "a poet"
who may never before have seen a poet,
seems in need of an answer to his question,
an answer I do not have, yet I answer:
I may not know where an idea comes from;
perhaps for days a phrase repeats itself,

perhaps a title, words which, isolated,
lack all meaning ("blue plums"); or situations
present themselves which seem, somehow, imbued
with those lights, half-lights, shadings, which address you
intimately, beyond all explanation,
whispering in your ear of resonance,
promising difficulty, complication.
I am able to glimpse, half-glimpse, its contours,
feel the weight it displaces (dimly, vaguely).
I am moving from darkness into darkness,
from mystery to deeper mystery;
what I see seems no plainer, seems no clearer,
the deeper I go, than it seemed, but rather
infinitely more complicated, darker.
If my answer succeeds in making nothing
simpler than it was, fails, utterly fails,
at illumination, it will convey
an approximation of my own state.

The third child smiles, nods her head up and down,
this way and that, assenting, acquiescing,
wanting me to agree, needing to hear
I, too, the poet, too, "always loved poems."
I am unable to confess that to her.
To the nodder I say: I did not love them
for what may well have been too long a time.
Apart from jingles we were taught at school,
I did not know just what a poem was,
what poetry might be. Only much later,
having by will, with effort, I suppose,
struggled to lead myself directly to it,
to bring myself to it, at last confront it
(convinced, I now suspect, I needed, needed,
to know what poems were, or poetry),
applied myself—what philosopher said

"It is all a matter of application"?—
read poet after poet, some too facile,
some too windy, some few whose lines I cherished,
those who drew me closer and closer to them.
I have not, I admit, "always loved poems,"
but those I came to love I live with, fiercely.

To the fourth child, sitting cross-legged before me,
light-haired, green-eyed, quite puzzled, Lady Wisdom
in a reflective mood, sensing which questions
beg to be asked, which never need be asked,
wanting, as any bright child wants, to know
why what I have been reading are called poems
(rather than maps, or cats, or inundations),
I convey, once more, doubt, uncertainty.
These are poems because I call them that,
because, when I think of them, I think "poem."
Should it please you to call them something else,
cucumbers, avocados, I accept that:
what you will name a poem is a poem,
becomes a poem, in the act of naming.
If this seems arbitrary to you, lacking
precision, the sheer weight of scientific
provability, it will have succeeded
in translating something of our dilemma.
We begin in ignorance, move through darkness
into the darkness, end in ignorance.
Poems are that, precisely: expeditions
mapping terrain where we have never been,
the landscape of the country of our blindness.

The fifth child, wearing white shorts and a smile
from here to there, and past that, wanting neither
the feel of things, their tone, their texture, nor
the consolations of exactitude,

statistics which, in time, attach themselves
to the object, whatever its name, under
scrutiny at the moment, asks my favorite
(as though that mattered), could as well have asked
the exact height and weight of each, how many
teeth each possesses. This is my response:
After completing "A," I liked it, liked it
better, perhaps, than what had come before it;
but when "B" seemed to drive a little further
into the dark surrounding it (a progress
meager, at best, those slow, minute advances
barely perceptible at such close range),
"A" was replaced by "B," however briefly.
Now I feel about "B" that it may have said
too much and, at the same time, said too little,
went not as far as, once, it seemed to go,
not as deep as perhaps it might have gone.
Each poem seemed, just finished, what I wanted,
thought I wanted; viewed from this distance, middle-
ground, back-ground, none seems what I had intended.

The sixth child blinks his eyes, swivels his head,
left to right, right to left, then rolls his tongue,
smacks his lips, makes a sound one-part delight
to one-part sheer boyish anticipation.
In the light of the values he assigns,
fails to assign, reminded once more of
the place of words, the homelessness of words
("Words, in the end, words alone, are what matter,"
that philosopher said, or might have said),
I feel it necessary to respond:
Ice cream? Of course there will be ice cream later,
more flavors than you knew existed, cookies
shaped like cottages (plumes of chocolate coiling
from crumb-top chimneys), candied apples, plum tarts.

By the time the desserts are brought and passed
(I suggest this for your consideration,
no more than that, one possibility
among the many which may offer themselves),
what you have heard (and, hearing, felt) may well seem
more astonishing than the crisps, the pastries,
the butterscotch napoleons, the rum balls,
mocha parfaits, coconut wafers, jam cakes,
the goblets of vanilla-laced-with-mangoes,
brought on trays from the pantry. One can know that
only at the conclusion, having sampled,
one by one, what was deftly laid before you,
poems read, plates passed, music heard, half-heard,
a judgment reached, or not reached, a choice made.

The seventh child addresses principles
fundamental, it would seem, to the context.
This seventh child has learned what I have not:
how not to be seduced by strains of music
glimmering in the words, above, beneath,
by floats, delights, whips, fizzes, freezes, sundaes,
concern for logic, reason, meaning, order,
for the demands of shapeliness, proportion.
He scans the sky with those dark eyes, he calls
a bird by its true name (a "ring-tailed swallow"),
he claims to hear the pounding of the surf,
the sweep of rain across the dazzling air,
although the sea lies days and nights from here
and storms have not been forecast for tomorrow.
I answer awkwardly, and yet I answer:
I hesitated when it was proposed
I read to you from poems I had written,
not because I would have denied you music,
not because I would not have had them touch you,
could they have touched you, but because my dreams

now seem the subject, have become the subject.
To read these poems to you is to tell you
what I dream, what my name is, who I may be.

Last night I dreamt a poet read to children,
seven children, each of whom asked a question
having, for the most part, to do with poems.
The lines the poet read were his responses,
his attempts at responses, to those children;
each of his answers asked more than it answered.
The poet wore my face, his clothes were my clothes,
the voice was mine, pitch, range, inflection, timbre,
the dream-words in that dream-speech were these words.
I was the man who stood before them reading,
you were the children, you, the seven children.
These were the lines I dream-spoke, line by line,
this was the poem, this, the very poem.

THE FERRY

Matthew Brady: Deck of the gunboat Hunchback *on the James River, May 5, 1864–February 23, 1865. Originally a New York City ferryboat, the* Hunchback *was purchased by the Navy in 1861 and armed with two guns. Because of its shallow draft, the gunboat was continuously used throughout the Civil War.*

Only in this man's head, and only there,
is the Civil War to be fought this morning,
if it is to be fought at all, one gathers,
this banjo-player, this maker of music,
bringer of music, this man for whom chanties,
folk airs, songs of the day, old hymnals, war tunes,
are wholly consolation, some reprieve,
however meager, partial, temporary,
for those few hours before darkness of evening
bears down across his shoulders, charged with omens,
burdened with strangeness now surpassing strangeness,
utterly haunting in its depth, shade, weight,
this banjo-player whose eyes now betray
(betraying much too well, too nakedly,
Mr. Brady may by now have concluded)
inconsolable sadness, vast, complete,
sadness overwhelming in its dimensions,
this strummer on whose knotted, black-skinned face
some unnameable fever of exhaustion
rages, works its way, has in fact already
worked its way, spread its damage, seared its mark,
the devastation too immense to say,
too desolate, too anguished, total, final,
sprawled on the deck, both legs straight out before him,

centered precisely in the grouping, foreground,
placed in the first row of successive rows
arranged behind him to the cabin deck,
magnet, linchpin, focus of our attention
(Mr. Brady's, as well?), just to his right
a man one guesses serves as the first mate,
a whistle on a rope around his neck,
to his left a portion of anchor cable
as thick as a man's leg, perhaps, or thicker,
taut on the weathered planks stretching to starboard,
plunging beneath the surface of the James,
beyond where we have been allowed to see.

Wheezing like the ferryboat it once was
(the crossing from Manhattan to the city
of Brooklyn, back from Brooklyn to Manhattan,
schooners from England, France, loading, unloading,
sugar, cinnamon, spirits, pelts, hides, textiles,
the twin ports thriving, both cities expanding,
spreading into farms far afield, uptown,
cobbles being laid in the avenues
leading to and from the commercial district,
boards hammered, nailed, cornerstones laid, dust, dust,
dust everywhere, horses' flanks, coach wheels, skirt hems),
its list visible some degrees to portside,
bobbing on what must have been river water
muddy, roiled, oil-slicked, more than anything
unquiet, though a glimpse of it eludes us,
the vessel rides at anchor for however
long Mr. Brady says he needs, or may need,
to do whatever he has come to do,
the crew piped from belowdeck by the first mate,
whistle on a rope dangling from his neck,
their chores, for the time it shall take, postponed,
the boat almost successful in its efforts

to escape its origins as a ferry
but for those certain tell-tale signs, not yet
wholly eradicated, Mr. Brady,
in his discretion, chooses to ignore,
determines, in the process, we not see.

Mr. Lincoln, this morning, has been touring
the battle lines one hundred miles from here,
the field hospitals, the administrator
guiding him, from the corner of his eye,
observing (the man dare not stare, look closely;
could it be what he saw or thought he saw?)
the President brushing tears from his cheek
(almost surreptitiously, he had thought),
viewing the mangled limbs, the bandaged head wounds,
improvised dressings streaked with grime, with blood,
of the young, bearded Seventh Infantry,
cot after cot, row after shattered row,
ward upon makeshift ward, camped out on ground
so dark, so dry, so obdurate, so burdened,
the President, should he have suddenly
dropped to his knees, whether in myth or fact,
beat his fists in the dust on which he kneeled,
would have fractured those long, pale, slender bones,
the thin, bare hands, with which the earth was struck,
only a low moan heard (thought?) to escape him.

None of the crew assembled is seen smiling
(one would not want otherwise, not expect it
otherwise, given what we have been given),
which does some proper justice to the moment
not available in a "composition,"
a look, a pose, another portrait-taker
might have requested of them, wished, imposed;
those whose feet we can see, but for the strummer,

lack shoes, not having had sufficient time,
perhaps the inclination, to don boots.
One of the crew holds a pipe in his mouth;
another, seen straddling the anchor cable,
bears a knife in his hands with which to whittle
something useful, or something beautiful—
remote, obscured, as yet to be determined—
relative to his nature or his need.
To the left, one of the rows to the rear,
a sailor holds a fuzzy, white-haired dog
within the circle his enfolding arms make,
its coat so thick it all but shields its eyes,
no more than a puppy, in fact, but holds him
with such tenderness in the cradling, such
gentle affection in the fondling, such
devotion in the nuzzling, such regard,
the circle of those arms at once so wide,
so intimate, encompassing, the puppy
peering out from that haven so content
(as though there were nothing more he might wish for,
nothing that had not already been granted),
so supremely comforted, sheltered, warmed,
so domestic, so blissful, the arrangement,
it almost seems the crew, receiving orders
moments ago, perhaps, is sailing home,
cannon fire now silenced, the war ended,
the James soon to be cleared of scuttled vessels
littering it, near shore, far shore, mid-channel,
rather than steaming for a night assault
on the coastal battery miles downriver.

Beside the sailor cuddling the white dog,
to the right, stands the man one takes to be
the navigator in the absence of one:
a chart is spread before him, which he peers at

with all the seriousness one expects
the navigator to bring to the task,
with all the poetry as well, perhaps
(though that, one understands, will not concern
those in command, not at all, not at all),
measurements, angles, depths, widths, distances
merely approximated from the deck,
the tints shading the river (sunset, moonrise),
the deep deceptions all things predicate
in combination with what lies unmet,
unseen, unknown, unpredicted, unfathomed,
reef, shoal, swamp, mudflat, siltage in the channel,
a draft too shallow for the proper clearance,
too narrow, short, too hazardous, the weight
of armature doubling the ferry's list,
twenty millimeter emplacements, broadsides,
the passage (turn, coast, brake, reverse, cut engines)
difficult, treacherous in the extreme,
unlikely even if negotiated.
The navigator holds his chart and peers,
this carpenter, this farmer, this horse-breeder,
navigating his way as best he can,
provisional, tentative, unproved, frightened,
navigation suddenly thrust upon him
at some last moment, some last, desperate moment,
the man one thinks of as true navigator,
true navigator, helmsman, steerer, peerer,
shoal-treader, reef-detector, fathom-sounder,
felled, cast ashore, wounded on a night run
against a coastal battery downriver,
the assault futile, fatal, half the crew
butchered, maimed, left for dying, decimated.

On the deck called the cabin deck, positioned
a level, one short flight, above the sailors,

aft of the dimness swamping the main deck now
where the crew, this morning, has been assembled,
first mate, banjo man, dog man, navigator,
stand those, seven or eight, wearing dark jackets,
white muslin blouses, soft felt, wide-brimmed hats,
seven or eight nonmilitary men
being transported somewhere south of here,
destination unknown, mission obscure.
They seem lighter than the crew (Mr. Brady's
handiwork—backlight, forelight, wide lens, cropping—
but, equally, what the men offer, too,
what they have brought here, travel with, begin from):
attitude, posture, bodies, faces, mood,
casual, almost, almost debonair,
seven or eight gentlemen, languid, leaning
against the rigging, lounging as one lounges,
would lounge, on a small cruise, a bright day, summer,
a long, lazy, leisurely day's excursion
downriver, back, a mere jaunt, nearly longing,
it would seem, to be shown in their best light,
pictured to their advantage, almost posing,
various multiple, unspecified,
unspecifiable, commercial interests
awaiting them, all transactions suspended
until, today, tomorrow, their arrival
south of here, north, abroad, everywhere, nowhere,
contracts signed, papers sealed, documents filed,
partnerships to be formed, already formed,
mergers drawn, not drawn, letters of intent
drafted, not drafted, lines of credit, tenders,
back rooms, front rooms, rooms barely rooms, offices
barely offices, hovels, tents, enclosures,
trench in a field, shack in the woods, foul mud ditch,
nickel lunches, cigars, spitoons, firm handshakes.

*

Mr. Lincoln, this morning, some one hundred
miles from where Mr. Brady trips the shutter,
caps the lens, waits, one last time grips the plate,
on the deck of a gunboat in mid-channel
of the James, the day clear (raw? overcast?),
blackbirds jamming the sky (hints? warnings? omens?),
the ground on which he stands (kneels? falls?) lush, grassy
(pitted? burned? scarred? wholly lost?), has been poring
over maps of the front line in the War Room
(a title which, at one time, could amuse him—
so self-important, so grand, so pretentious—
no longer, aides attested, quite amused him),
retreat, advance, the situation fluid,
the fluidity sheer chaos imposes,
shaking his head, muttering in his beard
to the effect that nothing he conceived of,
nothing, nothing any man might conceive of,
could justify such hate, such slaughter, nothing.
The young captain, Artillery, beside him,
standing till now at respectful attention,
freshly shaven, boots polished, buttons gleaming,
impeccably turned out, bright ginger mustache
clipped that very morning in expectation
of a visit, rumored, by Mr. Lincoln,
bearing sheaf after sheaf, campaign maps, to him,
sheaf by sheaf, map by map, page upon page,
bearer of sheaves, turner of pages, map man,
saw the President's hand shake on the parchment,
a momentary spasm, a slight tremor,
the quiver of the middle finger, passing—
in perhaps thirty seconds it had left him—
turned to him, partly turned, as the young turn,
not yet knowing how or where they might turn:
Mr. President, with all deference,
what of what one thinks right, Sir, what of justice?

Mr. Lincoln raised his eyes, studied him
over his rimmed bifocals, just-buffed boots,
silver buttons catching the light, pink cheeks,
ginger hairs groomed, each hair, to the same length,
the captain's eyes serene, unclouded, gray-blue:
The single right, young man, the single justice,
is for men to be what they can be: human,
the tone stern, not unkind, a father's tone
addressing a child too young, too impatient,
for understanding to have come to live with.

The war, then, is to be resumed this morning,
whether in this man's head or in a field
no victory, no poetry, redeems,
this plucker, picker, strummer, music-maker,
black banjo man, cook, hauler, fitter, stoker,
playing, his legs thrust out, on the main deck
improvised tunes (something beautiful? useful?)
extolling Mr. Lincoln's wisdom, courage,
this Sixteenth President of Our Republic,
praises in tribute to his wife, his sons,
scenes from the life, scenes from the war, dream scenes,
prayers, sermons, litanies, pleas to God.
(Strengthen him, that he bear what he must bear,
this great, good man, our brave, good Mr. Lincoln.)
It is time for them to be under sail,
almost time, a tide lifting, almost lifting,
a wind up, drifting from some landward, distant
conglomeration glimpsed too poorly, dimly,
to decipher now (sand? mud? marsh? swamp? scrub?),
called, on the chart, Commonwealth of Virginia,
dependent on the navigator's judgment,
his estimate of drift, displacement, light
(though, untested, he may well be reluctant
to have decisions such as these thrust on him),

Mr. Brady ready, seemingly ready,
to take his leave, bid his farewells, be lowered
to the two-man tender bobbing to portside
waiting to ferry him to the far shore,
the farther shore, the farthest shore, Virginia,
Virginia, looming misty, insubstantial,
Virginia, ghostly, half-seen, half-imagined,
speck on the estuary, dune scrub, marsh grass,
having finished the thing he came to do,
nearly finished, having had his hand clasped
by the first mate, departing, perhaps even
(one can fairly picture it, pictures it)
having himself asked the man with the banjo
if he might shake his hand, extend his thanks
for the music the man made when he boarded,
during the time it took to take their portrait,
folk airs, songs of the day, old hymnals, war tunes,
sitting before him strumming, picking, coaxing
something, something so weary, haunted, piercing,
from cat-gut string, warped boards, a plank of walnut,
its fragrance, black-skinned, fierce, lashing the air,
almost carrying to the farther shore,
the farthest shore, Mr. Brady debarking,
tucked in a folio beneath his arm
the plate, this plate, this banjo man, this one-time
ferry crossing to Brooklyn now a gunboat
nightly slipping downriver on the James
to do what damage it was meant to do,
this wheezer, lurcher, lister, this old *Hunchback,*
rope ladder put down, starboard, Mr. Brady
touching ground, almost touching ground, on ground
seemingly, from this distance, less than ground,
not wholly ground, and yet not wholly water.

FRENCH

For Joseph Gabriel

It could as well have been Danielle Darrieux's
diamond earrings, faceted, resplendent,
shimmering in the goblet of Chablis
(all gorgeous squills, all dazzling iridescence,

all fateful portents of the lights to come,
the life to come, Flaubert, Proust, the French for it)
set on the vanity by the maidservant
in attendance, an entrance, a retreat,

muffled across those mythic, antique carpets
which may, may not, have lain at Stendhal's feet,
a girl nineteen, hair bee-hived, deferential,
unobtrusive, there when her mistress rang,

just then, otherwise occupied belowstairs,
out of view, seldom thought of, never dreamt of
(not that we lacked concern, or looked away),
a life, lives, of which we glimpsed little, nothing,

given, stage center, at such vanities,
worshipped by lights, by lenses, soft, French, true,
pressing steadily forward, step by step,
glance by glance (an advance on one thing: grammar),

in that long campaign to seduce the camera,
Danielle Darrieux herself, arrayed in gems.
It could as well have been, in time, that gesture
as she gazed at the mirror propped before her,

fastening, first, one diamond to a lobe,
then the other, with such deliberation,
a dedication so contained, so private,
the attention she paid so fixed, so French,

turning, half turning, this way, that, front, sideways,
peering into the mirror, peering, peering,
asking the glass to move, be moved, catch fire,
to cry out once, just once: Perfect, oh perfect!,

it very nearly equalled, so it seemed,
the pleasure she gave, was to give, when, shortly,
gown smoothed, a hair, two hairs, tucked into place,
earrings secured, waves of light falling from her,

she rose, consenting, finally, to speak,
to coax the language into grammar, syntax,
invent the French, bestow on Fifty-eighth Street,
river to river, one end to the other,

light such as light has not since been bestowed:
murmuring, late, into the telephone
some stunning Oui, the perfect Oui, as though
it were her lover's ear in which she murmured,

which it was (he had called: Come now, I need you),
that one Oui, merely Oui, nothing more, Oui,
instructing the maidservant not to wait,
merely to leave a light, she would be late.

My education took place at The Paris
on Fifty-eighth Street, off Fifth Avenue,
its walls pale silver, gray, burgundy seats
tilting back should slight pressure be exerted,

downstairs a lounge where, during intermissions,
demitasse would be sipped from Limoges cups,
poured by young women chirping French, each wearing
blue and white bellboy suits with bellboy caps,

scenes from Watteau, vistas from Fragonard,
spilling across pale silver and gray walls,
tableaux beneath the willows, under elms
no more than faint green traceries, each drama

of flirtation, pursuit, spelled out before us,
maiden, consort, chaperone, garden meetings,
hushed confidences, ladies behind fans
almost swooning with ardor still concealed,

a fluttering of breeze, a splay of sun,
a whippet on a leash studded with garnets,
a swoop of hem, a show of ankle, hay-scents,
a filtering of French light through the leaves,

wherever one turned, half-turned, the perfume,
rich, thick, immensely sweet, of assignations.
Birds braid the startled air with music, flight,
the meadow burns with saxifrage, mint, saffron,

a gelding dreams, from the brush a lone rabbit
sings sweetly in the cadences of rabbit,
the cod cradle the sea, wild grouse build nests
in the tall grass, geese gambol, God is good.

I lived those weeks and months deep in The Paris
on Fifty-eighth Street, off Fifth Avenue.
I am fifteen that winter, not a moment
too soon to have been brought, in that long, slow,

unnecessarily difficult fashion
peculiarly my own, to understand
(approaching it from ignorance, not wisdom)
what it meant, might mean, not to live with French.

Deprived that year, devoid, bereft, one suffered
the fate of all those born to poverty:
one ached, fell mute, limped, made do, lived impaired,
persisted, in no sense, no sense, prevailed.

Even from the sixth row, poor, drenched with darkness,
condemned to sit without the gift of tongues,
a fifteen-year-old, blinded by Chablis,
by language, gesture (the world seen as gesture,

not duration), by Stendhal's mythic carpet,
by waves of lamplight beating, slowly, dimly,
into those corners yet unmapped, untrammeled,
grew drunk on earrings, whispers, Danielle's *Oui*.

It could as well have been Gérard Philippe
giving all, more than all, for love, for France
(even, one hoped, one dared to dream, for syntax),
crooning Baudelaire to the dance-hall lovelies

between sets, some point midway from the tango
on one side to the fox trot on the other
(squandered on them? you ask; not in the least:
nothing spoken in French, that year, was wasted)—

a strange one, never having a dance ticket,
appearing night to night, desiring only
to speak of just one thing: the soul, man's soul,
spending nothing, never buying us drinks—

girls from the Fourth Arrondissement, that highly
disreputable district on the outskirts
("the wrong side," as the swells in Clichy put it),
squatters' shacks, scrap yards, trash heaps, slaughter houses,

cold, nondescript flats where mobsters holed up
until the heat was off, drank, swore, smoked reefers
bought from boys who patrolled the Arab quarter,
back rooms where the failed suicides could hide,

dim flotsam of junked cars, abandoned lives,
half-lives, railway crossings no longer crossed,
trestles eaten with rust, rain slamming harder
here than elsewhere in Paris, when snow fell,

should snow fall, all day falling, with those certain
vaguely ominous, obscure blue-black tinges
stippled across its underside, forbidding,
night coming down too early, or too deeply,

neither, in such alleys, a prospect longed-for,
a consummation relished, a duration
(the world as gesture, rather than duration?)
"unendurable," as Gérard Philippe sobbed.

That education took place at The Paris
on Fifty-eighth Street, some thirty-six steps
(take the turn, count them) off Fifth Avenue,
that street from which, at fifteen, certain mornings,

clear, impossibly clear, momentous mornings
one's life seemed to wait at the next corner,
the next, the next, shining, welling with promise,
one would swear one could almost smell the Bois,

warmed by the sun lapping the beggars' quarter,
lit, late, by contexts of illumination,
hauntings, exactitudes, exfoliations,
left burning by the servant for her mistress.

(I shall be late, she told the maid, quite late;
leave a light burning for me, do not wait.
I said unto the lamp: burn not so brightly.
I said unto my life: thou need not wait.)

Gérard crooned Baudelaire; Danielle donned earrings;
the mobsters quit their flats to stroll the parks;
the boulevards grew beautiful with women;
French clear as water issued from their mouths.

(Gérard is gone. Danielle may be ensconced
in a small boutique on the Riviera,
the winters almost kind there, deaf, arthritic,
beating on the steam pipes—more heat! more heat!—

when seen seen once a week in the high season
advancing on the Villefranche bingo parlor
on the arm of a young man—sleek, quite blond,
wearing two gold necklaces—her companion,

as beautiful, perhaps, as she had been,
in some former life a cabana boy
to rich Americans at St. Tropez.
When asked what she remembers of those years,

Gérard, the earrings, Stendhal's carpet, *Oui*,
the France that was, the France that never was,
she rubs her thighs, cries once more: heat! more heat!,
sighs "Oh, these knees will cause me grief today.")

I am fifteen that year. March at The Paris,
miraculously, dawns mild, scented, clear,
the fruit trees bloom, the buds break into blossom,
Central Park, one block north, looms like the Bois,

crones from the Fourth Arrondissement wear crowns,
tiaras, ride a coach to the masked ball
drawn by serpents and beasts fluent in French,
spouting Ronsard, Villon, disport themselves

as though they were princesses, which they are,
were, may have been, may be, hope still to be
(all of it is possible, lovelies, all:
time, in time, will prove gesture, not duration),

wake the sleepers, enter the darkened suburbs
crying light, light, more light, no end to light
(I spoke unto the lamp: burn not so brightly.
I spoke unto my life: thou need not wait),

enchant the air with singing, with pure song,
dust gold leaf through such winter-matted hair
it takes until late summer to untangle,
arrive, arrive, arrive, no matter where.

THE HOME

I am wearing a pale silk lounging robe
the color of lake water glimpsed at dusk,
relic, it may be, of a life before this
of which no recollection, none whatever,
has survived, the sash once girdling the waist

confiscated the day I entered (laces,
ropes, belts: potential self-inflicted weapons),
wandering the corridors of The Home,
medallions of a previous campaign,
few but sterling, fastened to a lapel.

Outside, some trees bear the indignities
of the years of a long life—weather burn,
sun scald, leaf canker, trunk scars, root mold, rot—
with a degree of patience and composure
utterly moving, wholly to be envied.

Visitors, in winter, are few, if any.
The drive takes long, lies far; most of the maps,
whether by inadvertence or design,
have routes misplaced, or landscapes rearranged,
or roads which should lead somewhere leading nowhere,

turning back on themselves, ending in woods,
thwarted at that point a road should begin,
a chaos of unspeakable proportions,
a deliberate effort to mislead,
confuse, efface, distract, one more attempt,

part of a master plan, one rumor has it,
meant to discourage future expeditions,
holidays, Sundays, with their bleak reminders,
risky at best, of the past, of the human,
all one felt, suffered, who one was, may be.

Tea is brought at three-thirty, a young girl
with long red-gold hair, flushed cheeks, County Mayo
lacing the "Lemon? Sugar? Cream?" she speaks,
when she speaks, and pale gray-green eyes which seem
always needing not to encounter yours.

The custodian, particularly
those days snow falls, does his job, I must say,
to perfection, setting the thermostat
between seventy-six and seventy-seven,
keeping it there even after the dark falls,

when we dream (some still dream), walk in our sleep,
track the moon in the course of its ascension,
never tampering with it through the night,
those hours when need of warmth is most acute,
more so than I can bring myself to say.

From the west wing, where the kitchen lies wedged,
the stench of turnip overtakes the mornings,
the fumes of cabbage swamp the afternoons.
One knows, unfailingly, what lunch will offer,
what the dinner platter is bound to bring.

(The cabernet bouchet will not be poured
nor the wine of intimacy decanted;
no candles grace the disinfected tables.
Some small details still, darkly, pulse with light.
We all wish we were something we are not.)

Hard by that field where seven trees stand guard,
so touchingly heroic, bearing witness,
grackles and starlings search the brush for berries,
finding nothing, but nothing, to sustain them.
The undergrowth blooms fiercely, but with sorrow.

There are days, skies thick, choked, arrows of rain
glazing to sleet, the panes set in the dormer
starting to rattle, tugging against frames
bloated, warped, too loose to accommodate them,
I reach into a pocket of the robe,

stripped of its fringed cord for—their word—"safekeeping,"
withdrawing a small square of paper, folded
so many times, done, undone, done, refolded,
it has come by now to resemble lace,
its intricacies worked, reworked, dense, varied.

It is, or was, a letter, the hand your hand,
written in a language by now forgotten
(suffused, no doubt, with a music once crucial),
in which I was perhaps supremely fluent,
even (I say this difficultly) gifted,

a tongue from elsewhere, some great distance from here,
one neither heard nor spoken since, years, decades,
and for which I have no use any longer
in this life of a lost past, in the middle
of grounds flowering with one crop, one only,

and that profusely, year-round, year-round, one,
weather and season of no consequence,
skies choked, roads thwarted, a girl's eyes averted,
a life eloquent with preoccupations,
teeming, quietly, with the emblematic,

turning on these if, in fact, it should turn,
mapless, sashless, bordered by thermostats
on one side, fumes of cabbage on the other,
haunted by trees which stand guard, bearing witness,
trunks scarred, limbs hacked, visions swarming with grackles.

(Desolation takes its seat at the table
beside us, bright-eyed, waiting to be fed,
raucous, intrusive, thrusting out its plate,
famished for turnip root and hearts of cabbage.
I subsist on another diet: lace.)

It is strangely comforting, afternoons,
the starlings leaner by the hour, the grackles,
desperation unmitigated, wasting,
the others dozing in the hall, the small panes
for the moment at rest, the kitchen quiet,

to hold your letter, merely hold it, no more
(some last, small wounds still, dimly, throb with life),
ink faded, paper yellowing, torn, streaked,
what words remain, words I once knew, now foreign,
tone, nuance, pitch, too late to be retrieved.

Understanding nothing of what it tells,
even less of what, once, it might have told,
its perfume lost, its music dissipated,
I turn it left, then right, over and over
let the lace burn, burn through and through, with light.

Unlike most of the cases here, committed
out of anger, from an excess of hate,
poisons, night to night, thickening the blood,
mine has been diagnosed as the reverse.
An immense calm settled on me. I loved you.

LINCOLN'S HAT

Whatever you may have been told, or not told,
whatever is implied, or not implied,
stated, if stated, firmly, perfect pitch,
however worthy or instructive reading
Lives of the Famous may be, as suggested,
biography will be to no avail,
none whatever. All we needed to know,
parched for that rain of intimacy, famished
for the food of bright, riveting detail
(the portion small but crucial, the detail
minor, perhaps, but telling, with the eyes closed,
half-closed, glimpsed at a distance, sumptuous,
so glittering we cannot take it in
adequately, at first glance, wide-eyed, close range),
everything that might have instructed us,
even possibly saved us, will be left out:
who the man was, may have been; if he dreamt,
what he dreamt; what the years were; what he longed for.
(Mornings, he preferred eggs soft in the center,
wanted his coffee strong, was drawn to flowers
not too dazzling, those just a bit withdrawn—
the ones, if anything, you must approach,
not those which beckon to you—liked those tunes
laced with "a goodly portion of true feeling,
sentiment, you might call it," favored women
not at all prepossessing, pallid, thin,
those who spoke seldom, shyly, if they spoke.
His skin had a dark, mottled cast—just shaved,
he looked as though he were unshaved—his feet ached,

he had calluses, grew ring warts, slept poorly,
tossed on a mattress much too meager, dreamt,
felt palpitations, waking, suffered headaches.)

Fact is what is presented us, not more,
the mere fact, or the plain fact, or the simple,
fact alone, which will tell us nothing, nothing.
Look, instead, to the edges, to the borders,
where a thing is itself but something more
(always somehow becoming something more),
to the peripheral, the inadvertent,
something no doubt at first glance partly missed,
or wholly missed, in our hunger to search
that face for clues, to take that map of anguish
(slowly, carefully) in one's hands and read it,
verse by verse, page by page, from end to end,
read it, read it again, and then again,
in the belief something may have escaped us
the first time, or the second, or the third—
the stains of perspiration on the shirtfront
(the walk long, the road dusty, the day hot,
the sun pouring its light, its angle steep,
the rows of headstones in the cemetery
glittering, blinding him, making him dizzy);
or the specific texture of the dust
gathering in the creases of his boots,
caked in the cross-stitch of the trouser cuff;
or, most remote of all, perhaps, the hat,
that hat by which, two blocks away, a stranger
might know, gait aside, who it was approaching,
who it was he might stop, pay his respects to
(Good morning to you, Mr. President.
I thought I recognized you from a distance.
I will let you be on your way, but know,
please know, we pray for you and wish you well

in doing what you will to end this bloodshed),
worn in all weather, almost an appendage,
an outgrowth of his body, of his life,
the hat known in the '60s as the stovepipe.
(Dear Mr. Lincoln, a child might have written,
the letter postmarked Quincy, Massachusetts,
scrawled on sheets torn from a penmanship tablet,
When I asked Momma why you wear a hat
which seems to all but hide your face beneath it,
she allowed, as she did not know the answer,
I might put the question direct to you,
and so I do, meaning no disrespect.
My three little brothers, Momma and me
are of one mind in this—we take true pride
in you as President. You are a good man.
Yrs. truly. P. S. Momma says to tell you
Poppa is fighting with the Union forces
at Petersburg and he thinks likewise too.
We remember you each night in our prayers.)

The blackness of it is what strikes you first,
as black, say, as his beard, or as his boots;
as black as the sky on the ride from Springfield
on the night-coach, the trees luminous, wind
spreading its rumors through the leaves, the smell
of burning heavy on the air, pale smoke
ascending (guns? flames?) in the distance, almost
imperceptibly, sleep not possible,
the route circuitous, the lurching fierce,
the axles rusting, the grinding incessant,
the motion, back, forth, this way, that, hypnotic,
one by one the passengers taking ill,
stammering, bathed in sweat, feverish, retching;
as black as the frock Mary took to wear
in those late years (the doors slammed shut, barred, bolted,

the staircase to third-story rooms cut off,
the trays refused, left untouched on the floor—
poison everywhere, in the corners—mirrors
shattered, those not shattered covered with muslin,
those not covered with muslin turned to walls
long since stripped of bleak still lifes, bleaker landscapes,
the windows sealed with bedsheets, afternoons
filled with her silences, nights filled with worse—
dreaming, dreaming, gaunt shadows, visions, hauntings,
visits from those who, bringing the past with them,
are unwelcome—muttering to herself,
to him, of the frightful burden of evil
in the world, oh the weight of it, of darkness
falling, falling, forever falling, of how
no grief, no mourning, none, proves quite sufficient,
ever, to match the sum of all the losses,
those suffered yesterday and, worse, much worse,
losses yet to be suffered, still to come).
The blackness rises, rises slowly, straight up,
undermining those definitions, rising,
having to do with inadvertence, edges,
borders, peripheries, those preconceptions
we carried here with us, making us question
what part, biographer, is hat, pure hat,
pure real yet imagined hat, what part,
rising, rising, immense, blacker than black
(more than one knows what to do with), is Lincoln.

OLANA, SUMMER, 1872

About one hour this side of Albany is the center of the world, and I own it.
—FREDERIC EDWIN CHURCH

In the morning, as one visitor wrote, the house party "sat writing in different rooms on different Persian carpets with different pounded brass inkstands and different Oriental stuffs hung about on easy chairs of antique or artistic shape." As for the weather, it was "that real warm inland out-of-door weather, soft, not too hot, regular country, not at all seashorey, with a suggestion of muslins."

Lottie,
       A pause in the festivities here,
momentary, at best, I can assure you,
permits me now to write you this, dear Friend,
rather than choosing wholly to entrust
to memory all that one would entrust
of the views (quite unrivaled), the impressions
(splendidly unsurpassed), collecting in me,
through these weeks of the most astonishing
vistas, small dramas, reminiscences,
one heaped upon the other, fantasies
(each day a fresh one, so it seems) enacted,
reenacted, set forth, fleshed out, made real.
Had I within me such gifts as an author
most requires to make her presentation
in an absorbing fashion—style, perhaps,
refinements of technique, assuredly
not subject matter, which abounds, sufficient,
I daresay, to fill volume upon volume,
could one but put one's mind, one's whole mind, to it,

to this alone, in a manner one might call
singular, concentrated, undeflected—
I might do the scene justice, more than justice.
Yet I lack, equally, talent and patience,
and thus, dear Friend, I trust we shall make do
with whatever spills from this pen your Em holds,
meager, scattered, and dim as it may prove.

And to think I very nearly refused
(or was caused to refuse, might better state it)
Frederic Edwin Church's invitation
to come from Cambridge for a stay in August,
that I might visit with him at Olana.
He is a painter, from what I had learned—
there was no one I did not ask about him,
no one I did not turn to for details
(even the most trivial bore a meaning)—
the most famous one we have, I was told
by those much more conversant with the subject
than I am, or could ever hope to be.
I learned what names I could before I came,
Delacroix, Rubens, Titian, Giotto, that young
Frenchman of whom they speak at present, Degas,
so that, across the table from him, evenings,
on strolls through the gardens (I shall describe,
or shall attempt to, these surroundings for you,
this great house perched high on a precipice
with views of the Kaatskills and of the Hudson,
the next view more enchanting than the last),
I appear to Mr. Church, to the others
who have been asked here as his guests this summer,
less frivolous, less empty-headed, than
you and I, Lottie dearest, know me to be.

*

Father, I must say, took a dim view of it
(dimmer than dim, in all truth, renders it
with some greater fidelity, I fear)
from the start, though it is his Great-Aunt Nella
herself who knows Frederic Edwin Church.
In June he paid a call on her at Newport
where, among the daguerreotypes displayed
on the spinet in her wicker sun parlor,
he spied the one she keeps of me—hair quite long,
spilling across my shoulders, down my back,
in that bonnet, pale straw, wide-brimmed, I wore
summer-before-last to the Bedford Fair,
its sash tied in a bow beneath my chin.
He asked her if she thought I might enjoy
a visit to Olana. Write to her,
ask the girl yourself, Aunt Nella told him.
Tell her Father who you are, that you know me,
that you are quite a fine, upstanding man
(tell him Aunt Nella said that), husband, father.
Father, shortly thereafter, had this letter:
Dear Nephew, Frederic Edwin Church, it happens,
seems quite taken with that portrait of Emma
adorning the old spinet in my parlor
(who can properly blame him, what with those eyes,
that hair draped like a shawl about her shoulders,
that mouth a painter could not reproduce,
could not begin to hope to reproduce,
in a lifetime of sittings?). Let her visit,
should the man write to ask (I feel he shall),
permit the girl a taste of that great world
beyond, just beyond, where she may have traveled,
has had small opportunity to travel.
It is my conviction (I have long felt this)
Emma is someone who could flourish, flourish
and grow, given a soil which warms, which nurtures.

Let it begin here for her, let this be
(you, you alone, shall make it possible)
her debut, if you like, her introduction
to whatever makes a life fuller, sweeter.

Mother, for her part, knowing full well (better
than Father, need I tell you) what one's chances
are, or can be, should her summers be spent
in Cambridge, took a view somewhat less dim.
From a list of chaperones and companions
presented to them for consideration,
they fancied, without hesitation, Cousin
Georgina, second daughter of my Aunt
Caroline (Father's side), Georgina Steadman,
older than I, slender, quite tall, a spinster
(the Steadmans settled long ago in Springfield;
do you recall her brother, Cousin Brandon:
the Commonwealth Cotillion, last December?)—
a shy girl, really, somewhat lacking spirit,
on the plain side, I must say, withdrawn, quiet,
but, for all that, kindly, temperate-natured
("a stable influence" was Father's judgment),
not at all someone I should be reluctant
to entrust with a confidence, if need be.

Alice James had invited me to join her
in Europe (they had sailed, in May, for England),
but, a fortnight ago, her Mother sent word
Alice had taken ill, had been confined
to her bed with some ailment Mrs. James
seemed at a loss to specify. Poor Alice,
one thought the girl never very robust
(perched on down pillows in that narrow bed
of hers, in that house with a gabled roof
in Quincy Street, in a room on the third floor

at the end of a corridor bereft,
I can attest—"Alice's nerves," I was told—
of even the barest illumination,
where a wall slopes, slopes downward, floorboards creak,
and a glimpse of the street from the stained glass
set in the dormer comes back blurred, misshaped,
a hairline crack in the far corner splitting
the world in two should one, like Alice, view it
from that window, from that window alone,
propping, as she propped, notepaper on knees
—knees bonier than I can tell you, Lottie—
sun streaming through the fanlight in the attic,
tinting her face fierce purple, hair pure green,
letters from Harry, or from Willie, not so
much from her other brothers, heaped beside her,
strewn on the bolster, night-stand, blanket, sheet,
scattered like snow across the coverlet,
dropping to the floor, Alice—and no matter
whether it be morning, high noon, late evening—
penning responses: to Harry, in London,
or to Willie, wherever on this Earth
Willie had chosen, that year, to be off to),
not a girl, I daresay, with strength sufficient
to endure a tour of the Continent—
at the height of midsummer, in the bargain—
and all that shall entail. Her great good fortune
is that she travels with her brother Harry,
as familiar with those parts as with Cambridge,
having earlier toured there, and their Mother.
(Harry, since I speak of him, is the author
of some quite humorous, quite charming, stories—
do you take *Scribner's Monthly?*—although Father
refers to them as "watery," "anemic"—
very much the gentleman, his demeanor
more than a trifle influenced, one's guess is,

by those stays on the Continent: a flat
in London, nights at a box in the theatre
in the company, to hear Alice tell it,
of some tall, white-wigged, cinched-waist dowager
princess or other, late of Biarritz;
the heiress to a company whose ships
haul cargo to the Orient and back;
a Viscount's wife; one or two countesses,
Italian, French, their names tinkling like music,
with a title difficult to pronounce,
dating, no doubt, to the twelfth century.)
All thought of Europe must, I fear, be put off,
at least until such time as Mrs. James
sends word that all is well there. I suspect
it shall be not in London nor in Paris
I see our Alice next, but here in Cambridge,
when the Jameses return to Quincy Street.

The stage from Springfield was three hours late,
the road treacherous, heat intense, my saffron
crinoline coated hem to hem with dust.
At the Albany Station, two maidservants
in the employ of Frederic Edwin Church
met us in F. E. C.'s own private coach,
drawn by four horses, each pure, dazzling white.
The road meanders downhill through the valley,
a most leisurely, blossom-filled descent;
before Olana has been glimpsed, or half-glimpsed,
the glitter of the Hudson snares the eye,
green at cliffside, blue where the current stirs,
one hour's ride from the Albany Station,
a most pleasant ride, I might add, the views
matching, so F. E. C. claims, Europe's best views—
deep woods, sheer cliffs, the great river itself,
stands of oak, maple, hemlock, birch, pine, chestnut,

trees planted, mind you, by the man himself,
prospects which please, which, in truth, more than please,
the air smelling of fresh hay, of wild grapes,
balmy with summer, grass scents, country scents,
scents which bespeak the presence of the river
(the Hudson two miles wide here, Massachusetts
gleaming in one direction, in another
Vermont, Connecticut in still another,
the robin, hermit thrush, gray and red squirrels,
making themselves heard, spaniels, setters, donkeys
brought from Syria for the hills and paths here,
turtles, white cats, even a just-born owl,
abounding, gardens clipped, meticulous,
shaped with the care a sculptor might have taken,
the plantings various, the eye enchanted,
long rows and perpendiculars, light streaming,
order wherever one might turn, might not turn,
might well, perplexed, have contemplated turning,
yet a chaotic order, nothing fixed,
nothing that might not change, or be changed, nothing
Frederic Edwin Church might not wish altered,
might not improve upon, transpose, create.

It was Frederic Edwin Church himself
to greet us at the gatehouse on debarking.
Mr. Church, I shall tell you, has the most
delightful manner possible conversing,
initiating conversation, with young
women who come so far by coach from Cambridge,
the road poor, the heat fierce, their frocks grime-coated.
From beneath the blondest brow one might see,
the blondest, one might add, one hopes to see,
he closes the left eye, perhaps half-closes,
squints with the right, half-squints, proceeds to fasten
a steady, clear, consistent, blue-eyed gaze

at a location just south of one's chin
("How fair must be the air of Massachusetts,
that it offers us such comely young women"),
informing us dinner is served at seven
in a wing facing west (in truth, a terrace
overlooking the water, grazed by willows,
rays of the sun filtering through the branches),
that, when dessert and coffee shall be brought,
a steward passing snifters of plum brandy,
small cups of jasmine-scented Arab tea,
one can, with the glacé, see the sun set,
if, in the dark, one might be of a mind to—
fiery golds, pinks, purples, blazing crimsons.
Thereafter, and immediately so,
when the first stars make their appearance ("New
York State's very own stars, you may be certain,"
he boomed, making such declaration proudly,
as if they, too, were his, arranged by him,
just so, rising on cue when he decreed,
when Frederic Edwin Church cried: Rise, stars, rise),
would follow a display of pyrotechnics
devised in colors and configurations
by none other than our host, architect
of all on which the eye saw fit to gaze,
the lawns and parks sloping to river's edge,
the pond on which great white swans took to sail
so peaceably, with such grace, such pure languor,
the hills themselves, each rise, each elevation,
altered so that, in the painter's own words,
one might see better what there was to see,
the prospect, all prospects, thereby enhanced:
river, cliffs, woods, sky, dawns, dusks, fall of darkness.
Should he not have named his estate Olana
(meaning, in Arabic, Our Place on High),
I daresay Mr. Church might well have named it—

living, as the man seems to, for light, light—
Sunsets and Auroras, a phrase employed
repeatedly by him since our arrival,
spoken with fervor, his enthusiasm
marked, distinct, an outpouring of high spirits
all-encompassing, limitless, profound,
very nearly, one ventures to say, childlike,
trusting the term conveys to you the freshness
with which all things are viewed by him, the passion
for newness seizing him, by which he lives.

From another wing in this house with wings
more than one might account for on ten fingers,
one hears, at some distance, the revels starting—
the ladies stirring from their naps or, like
myself, having come from their correspondence,
the men from their cigars and who-knows-what talk—
indicating I must soon be off, Lottie.
Later, following dinner, there is planned
one of the divertissements Mr. Church
arranges every evening, various
pageants, parades, processions, what he terms
theatricals, little theatricals,
entertainments extending half the night,
fantasy's own fleshed-out embodiments
to divert guests, friends, family alike.
(F. E. C. is a man of great high spirits,
much given to imaginative frolic—
improvisational may best portray it—
with a mind most acutely analytic,
quick, keen, discriminating, and a taste
—might it better be called hunger?—for beauty
in whatever form or fashion it takes,
may, undivined by us, elect to take.
Aunt Nella calls it the painter's affliction,

claims it may be just for that I was asked here,
reason enough, to hear her tell it: beauty.)
To my extreme relief, all talk of painting
is in abeyance, night to night, at table,
with the ladies present. Such lofty discourse
seems to transpire later, among the men,
a subject about which, I shall confess,
I remain as unschooled as when I came.
(The ladies speculate upon the frock
Mrs. Ulysses Grant may choose to sport
at the First Lady's Spring Cotillion next year—
American? Parisian?—whether its style
prove traditional or, as rumor has it,
augur the future—fabric, drape, fit, cut—
talk which seems not to satisfy for long,
though one speaks for one's own taste, that alone.)

Each of us shall depict a princess (Persian)
waiting beneath the date palms, perfumed, veiled,
and the men (among them the Sturdevant
brothers, Ethan and Myles, who partnered us
through two or three reels at the Boston Christmas
hoedown and hayride; Ethan, dark, a student
in landscape portraiture with Mr. Church,
Myles, fair, the elder by two years, immersing
himself in aspects of the law, at Harvard)
bearded warrior chieftains, horsemen, princes
in burnooses, keepers of tented harems.
I shall be off now for a costume fitting—
one or two inches gathered at the waist,
Mrs. Thornton claims, is all I require
(F. E. C. has his own resident seamstress
on the premises—such a kindly woman)—
and to have the strap of my sandal stitched.
I have gone on much too long, I admit,

yet one cannot bring oneself to believe
Lottie shall scan this with less than fond interest,
trusting, as I do, that her tastes and mine
complement each other, balance precisely—
the cause, one of them, I hold her so dearly.

If, on your walks through Cambridge, you encounter
any member of the James family,
do kindly, if you will, send word at once.
One cannot wholly separate oneself
from the thought of dear Alice, of—despite
Mrs. James' reticence—what befalls her,
its portents for the future. Her good Mother
speaks of a "lassitude," a "listlessness,"
the "fragility" of her state. I cannot
claim, in all conscience, Lottie, to be versed
in the Mental Sciences nor conversant
with such modern practices and techniques
as the practitioners perhaps employ,
but I daresay Alice's maladies
seem, to my mind, not without a relation
to living in a house in which one brother
is an author and another a thinker—
even to draw breath at that dinner table
must have proved daunting for her, Henry Senior
himself discoursing on religious matters
(his manner quite as lucid as his sons'),
Harry on motive, meaning, instinct, feeling,
Willie addressing philosophic questions
(if G–d be vengeful, might we be the cause?),
Alice in that black, lattice-backed straight chair
glancing at father, brother, brother, father,
not knowing what to say, nor how to say it,
nor—this the worst of it—to what avail.
They are, I daresay, kind, most kind, to me,

exemplars, each, of extreme graciousness—
Harry, one might say, even deferential—
whenever I have come to call on Alice.
Yet, withal, one is hard put to imagine
anyone sitting, evenings, in that parlor
whose walls sway to the flicker of the glow-lamps
("Alice's nerves," remember: dimness reigns here),
matching, even struggling to match, a discourse,
a mode of discourse, some mere flimsy tissue
of words-strung-together, a conversation
so consistently charmed, weighty, high-minded,
so learned, proper, difficult, precise,
so relentlessly laced with passion, wit.

Frederic Edwin Church has written Father
asking if I might stay through mid-September.
(Father, I fear, shall not give his consent.)
To you alone, my Lottie, can one say this:
one finds oneself hard put to entertain
even the merest prospect of returning,
after Olana, to the life of Cambridge.
One shuts one's eyes, one holds one's breath, one whispers:
one need never ask for oneself again
should this be granted, this: let it not end.
Olana, Lottie, is some Paradise
on Earth, another Eden, some dream palace
in which what one most longs for, until now
anonymous, amorphous, for the first time
assumes a shape, a weight, utters its name.
Aunt Nella, Mother writes, requests of Father
that I pay her a visit next in Newport
("fresh from her triumph," Aunt wrote, "at Olana"),
yet few young people journey now to Newport,
and soon, too soon, it shall have been abandoned:

the cottages are closed, the ballrooms shuttered,
the galas spilling music to the dark
ended, the dancers fled, the music stopped
(even the gulls sound plaintive, mired in sand,
and, in autumn, Newport is sand, all sand).

Claire Chadwick writes she and her Aunt Vanessa
shall, in a fortnight, travel to New York,
Aunt Vanessa proposing to write Father
asking if I might venture there to join them,
suggesting I take rooms at their hotel,
The New Imperial, in Fourteenth Street,
the windows of whose suites, to hear Claire tell it,
front the greensward just recently created
at Union Square, in such proximity
to the fine shops, the music halls, the theatres
flourishing, Claire attests, that far uptown,
one, it would seem, need never, from the first day
to the last of one's stay there, hail a carriage.
I do not yet know what it is I shall do,
nor—more obscured—what Father may accede to
(one seems at odds with all present proposals
save one: prolonging one's stay at Olana),
but I assure you it is with affection
I think of you, of times past, with a full heart
I shall greet you when next we meet. Trusting
our friendship bears for you signification
equal to what it bears for me,
                                    Your Em

WILLIAM JAMES IN BRAZIL

According to Henry James, William set standards of intelligence, confidence, and common sense which daunted his siblings. Resisting his father's strong desire that he become a scientist, he pursued painting until adolescent study convinced him of his mediocrity. He next studied chemistry, and then anatomy and physiology under Harvard scientist Louis Agassiz. Still dissatisfied, he shifted to Harvard Medical School in 1864. During a collecting expedition to Brazil with Agassiz in 1865–1866, he contracted smallpox, which temporarily blinded him.

Dear Harry,
              It may be, may very well be,
to you, to you alone, I can confide this:
this blindness is not wholly to be dreaded,
though I suspect—and you shall understand this—
the reasons will have less to do with me,
most likely, and more to do with Brazil.
You, I daresay, would flourish here, would read
into this richness, no doubt, equal richness,
would find, at the least seek, a metaphor
which, to the last detail, might match the scene,
would take this lushness, this profusion, this
extravagance of color, scent, heat, light,
and make of it much more than most would make,
more than your brother Willie knows or cares to.

Cares to: that may state the truth of it best.
This loveliness (I am not blind enough
not to have seen loveliness when I saw)
seems to serve only to confuse me further,
cause dizziness, unsettle me, distract me

from what I thought my purpose was to be here.
(I came not for adventure, you remember,
not for diversion, not for the romance—
spurious, self-induced, in my belief—
with which travel, for others, seems imbued.)
The truth is I am unable to work,
unable to grasp the enormity
of this landscape, the life forms, dawns, the dusks,
unable to distinguish the horizon
from the sky, or the sky from the horizon.
Whatever forces (I cannot yet name them;
they resist, seem to resist, all attempts
at categorization) are at work here,
whatever factors (even clues seem lacking)
conspire to meet here to yield this "Brazil,"
all seems past my capacity to fathom,
to delve into, to wish to delve into.
Whatever definitions, I assure you,
the scientific mind arrives equipped with,
whatever, in the past, one may have known,
or thought one knew, whatever mere degree
of insight one possessed (marginal, brief),
is, or has been, or shall be, unavailing.
(I have, I must admit, some difficulty
even shaping its sound: *Brazil, Brazil.*)

You, with your taste for ambiguity,
symbol, drama of the interior,
nuance, half-tones, half-lights, glint of refractions,
private experience; you, with your passion
(misplaced passion, according to my view)
for layer upon layer, your insistence
on context, context, context, would quite thrive here,
would find wholly appropriate this setting,
this welter of extremes, of influences,

this disorder, this unremitting chaos.
The possibilities, the combinations,
possible combinations, seem unending,
their infinitude very much the cause
of this disquiet which has settled on me
("disquiet" does small justice to it, Harry;
it is an affliction as yet unnamed,
as yet, for that matter, unnameable).
There is nothing here, nothing in this climate,
which is simply itself, not something more,
which does not stand for something else or cannot:
the light, fierce, fierce, is more, I swear, than light
(even before this other blindness set in,
that was enough, more than enough, to blind me);
this heat punishes more than mere heat would,
falls, each day, like a curse, and not like weather,
rises from the fields like a visitation,
all dust-enshrouded, all vapor and shimmer;
and in the evening (nights are the worst of it),
when one might expect cooling, shade, reprieve,
when, at last, one might stand out in the open,
it is more than the dark that comes down, Harry:
nothing ceases, retreats, nothing relents,
all of it is much as it was, but more so;
mystery, rather than dissipating, deepens
(and when it does come down, even now, now,
I feel myself, even blind, almost shudder;
though I can see none of it, none, I shudder).

I suppose you might think of me as haunted,
which is most uncharacteristic of me,
as you well know. There are few facts to grasp,
or none, no statistics, no measurements,
which might anchor one to the world one lived in.
I am, perhaps for the first time, adrift,

cut from my moorings, like one of those creatures
in a story you have written, or shall write
(over and over, to my keen dismay),
one of those drab souls, bloodless, wholly juiceless,
from whom whatever life it—he?—possessed
has been squeezed, someone, Harry, whose existence
is thin, or beyond thin, thinner than thin,
his hold quite tenuous on solid objects
(and solidity need not be regarded,
as, I fear, you regard it—even by those,
like yourself, who address themselves, or would,
to not quite visible manifestations,
auras, to the not readily apparent—
as an enemy). There are worse fates, Harry,
than to live in a world not of one's making.

I think you know what it is I most want:
to have done with the work here, to return
to a life, to a self, known to me. I need
to have Brazil behind me, much behind,
so that one cannot view it short of turning,
short of looking back. (I assure you, nothing
could induce me to turn, then, to look back,
nothing, nothing whatever.) "When I get home,
I'm going to study philosophy all my days."
I know that now. Why I could not have known it
earlier quite defies my understanding.
I have, I feel, squandered too much, too much,
dallied too long with what seems not essential,
though it may have to do with being blind now,
with living in these parts, trying to live,
where whatever I touch eludes me, floats off,
vaporizes at a touch, the mere touch.

*

In the next letter I will send to you
that photographic portrait taken of me
by a man, a Brazilian here, who travels
through the back-country photographing native
tribes never seen before by other men—
wearing a trimmer beard, the little, round,
dark glasses, and the hat, your favorite hat
("plantation hat," you christened it), its wide brim
sweeping upward at both sides of the head
at, I daresay, a quite dramatic angle.
Agassiz claims it came out rather well,
distinctly South American, he calls it.

I wished to say a word about those chapters
from the novella sent a fortnight ago
and read to me the very week they came,
but the details must wait until next time.
Agassiz' secretary reads your letters
as well as whatever else you may send me,
writes my letters, as well, just as I speak them.
Already I may have (though I try not to)
taxed him, this afternoon, beyond all fairness.
Briefly, I say what I have said before,
which, as before, you must not hear too harshly:
I know no one your characters resemble,
by which I mean they seem, each, not quite human,
not sufficiently lifelike to quite warrant
such relentless speculation about them—
thoughts, motives, gestures, what lies past the words
they speak, beneath the words, beneath the text
you have provided for your readers, Harry.
I am unable to persuade myself
others exist on the exalted plane
where you insist, it seems, on placing them,
locations, to your loss, found on no map.

Possibly too much emphasis is put
on what they feel, and think, not what they do
(your characters, quite simply, do not *do*).
I have never known men and women like that,
nor would I care to. Have you? Would you wish to?
I state this with acute concern: you travel
too much into your own imagination,
too far into those areas unknown
to most of us and of import to few.
Might you not see your way to take a step back,
several steps, in the other direction,
devising characters not so obscure,
whose minds one finds accessible, less murky,
people whose reality one believes in,
for whom to be discreet (oh, your discretion)
is least of their concerns, preoccupations,
their motives, if not understandable,
explainable, made palpable, fleshed out?
You must, I beg you, no longer be tempted,
as you have been tempted, to undertake
exploration of that whole realm of shadows
you have been drawn to in such

                          I break off here.
Night has fallen; the old unease returns,
keeping quite scrupulously to its schedule.
(More, much more, than the dark comes down here, Harry.)
Agassiz' secretary has, I fear,
grown weary, after all he has been put through
this afternoon. Nothing I might have said here
diminishes, I hasten to assure you,
the high regard in which I hold you nor
the considerable importance to me
of your gift of solicitude, a rare gift,
and my sense of its presence in my life,

this for now sightless life. You might spare Mother
and Father the details of which I write.
(No need to worry them unduly, is there?)
They know simply (simply!) I have been blinded,
a blindness free, or so they trust, of pain.
(Would that I could believe, or claim, the same.)
That is enough. (Discretion, as I said,
is what you were born to.) Convey to Alice
her brother's deep, deepest, affection,

                                        Willie

THE DROWNING OF
IMMORAL WOMEN

Thingvellir, the Parliament Fields, where for almost a thousand years Icelanders gathered for reading of new laws, execution of criminals, and drowning of "immoral women."

One could never be certain what their crime was,
never understood what they had been charged with:
loving too much, loving too little, loving
not at all; living, or attempting to live,
close to risk, too close, chance, too much at stake
(a narrow ledge, the dark on either side,
bottomless, measureless, difficult, burdened,
the height precipitous, the drop forbidding);
curiosity, in some certain cases,
of a sort no longer fashionable
or (should fashion disclose too little, nothing,
of yearning, context, circumstance) no longer
deemed appropriate on the part of women,
immodest, disproportionate, in excess,
at some extreme even promiscuous,
unbridled, lacking taste: in sum, unseemly.
The morning may have been dim, gray, mist-shrouded,
just the day, one surmises, for a drowning,
for drownings, just the day, should one be placed,
should one manage somehow to place oneself,
uninvited, unseen, in a position
advantageous, you who would grasp it all,
to a consideration of such factors
as mist, frost, clarity, angle of vision,

sightlines, such nearness and such farness crucial
to the introduction of depth perspective,
with its attendant burden on dispassion;
just the day (and for reasons never asked,
never disclosed), from wherever it is
one has secreted oneself, to observe them,
half-naked, weeping, wounded, early, late,
hair undone, eyes betraying just that wildness
desperation encourages to flourish,
being led by seven impassive escorts
barefoot on stones, field after field of them,
to the arena of this windless plain
flooded with inlets of a half-seen sea
flashing its lights somewhere off in the distance,
making its way by degrees this far inland.

Lashed one to the other by the bleached sashes
tugging at the loops of their pastel bathrobes—
yellows, pinks, greens, startling in a seared landscape,
treeless and leafless, drained of color, passion—
(it was early knocks-on-the-doors came, early
members of the town council, seven, stood there,
rigid, stern-faced, nothing but their lips moving,
announcing what they had come to announce,
reading, in turn, from the text of the edict,
point by point, through a long night, hammered out
to unimpeachable specifications;
early to have come to grips with the nature
of what would be described as their transgressions;
too early, roused from sleep, to have had time,
each of them, to have struggled into house frocks,
even, most of them, to have searched for slippers
under beds, in the childrens' play-room, outside
where the dog, last night, hid them, the salt garden
where they cultivate, try to, work, work fiercely,

the long, clenched rows of utter fruitlessness),
they are being led, closer and closer—
a leading which will prove to be, must prove,
finally, their undoing—to the sea,
barefoot, tear-stained, their cries lashing the air
to small avail, the bruised hems of their robes
grazing the jagged stones on which they stumble,
hair disarrayed, no more so than their eyes,
their feet cut, bleeding, arms tied to their sides,
the long stench of derangement rising, rising,
a thousand years of it, thick, rancid, heavy,
having, as the edict would tell it, point
by point, page after page, "exhibited
tendencies" judged to be readily able
(one thinks of the irresolute, the young,
those whose choices, whose lives, still lie before them)
to "subvert," inadvertently or not,
the very "fabric" by which bands of men,
"men and women in consort," by agreement,
recognize themselves as "not less than human,"
not less, in time possibly more, much more
(these are their words, theirs, taken from the edict),
a recognition no "contamination"
of "ideas, example, speech, behavior,"
not a hint of it, shall be "countenanced,"
can be permitted to "infect," to "sully."

Where the sea floods the inlet, where the inlet
tastes of inlet but tastes, too, more of sea,
where the water, that fraction we glimpse of it,
has turned, now turns, to sky, sky on the brink
of becoming (and soon, soon, too soon) water,
their ankles feel the damp, are stung by salt,
their wounds leak color slowly on the tide,
their hems begin to soak, an inundation

wholly beyond the force of these strange waters
to depict, to articulate, to fathom,
engulfs, seduces, flays them, chills their bones,
the wading, this relentless movement seaward,
this progress (call it that) toward a drowning,
inch by raw inch, without pause, unabated,
continues, for as long as one can see
to the horizon, through this loathsome morning,
deeper and deeper, darker, wave by wave,
horizon sky, sky water, water staining
richly, rapidly, more pervasively,
this far north, so far, than one dare imagine.

FOR THE DARK ONES

One wanted, at the start, nothing so much
as to be able to sleep through the Eighties,
or so one thought when the man made his entrance.
(Who can he be, one asked, where had he come from?,
questions, perhaps to one's extreme advantage,

never resolved, never resolvable.
Where shall private begin and public end?)
Vain hope, it happens: anguish wakens us
at the moment we might wish least to wake,
choices never granted us to refuse.

Let it devolve on timing, as it must.
(Has the mindlessness been concluded? Are we
whole, do we come halfway to being healed?
Hands extended, late, in deep woods, the dusk
too pronounced to be altered, undone, turned back,

one eye scanning the sky, do we just stand there
crying, again, again, Come down, Come down,
knowing, knowing too well, what must come down?
How, how, one asks, is passion to be managed?
Name the thing concluded, the thing contained.)

Even beneath the snow the bears are climbing
slowly back into life through a hard winter,
a long, fierce clawing, paw by ice-fast paw,
sniffing fish after fish river by river
in their dream of resplendent mullet, salmon,

ecstatic in the falls, awash with glitter,
gripping their flesh in fabled, mythic, dream teeth.
Who can account for timing in these matters?
Despite our knowledge, pears begin to ripen
on the difficult slope beyond the sun,

not according to schedule, my dear, dark one,
a terrain inhospitable, forbidding,
soil unpromising, weather foul at best,
roots a conspiracy of aspiration,
tangled, murky, chaotic, dense, unsplendid,

too jammed, too labored, to come to fruition,
light, even hope of light, at last abandoned
(what is to sustain us against such losses?),
the sound wild fruit makes, frail, tentative warbling,
those small attempts at something close to music,

if not music itself yet, rising slowly,
plaintively, from the very heart of longing.
(Think of the route they travel on the journey,
thrusting blind in the dark, uphill throughout,
the cost of what they suffer to be here,

patience, frost, fever, scent, ultimate passion,
the frightful weight, the agony, of one
relentless, green idea in the mind,
suspended all the while before them, gleaming,
overriding, a singlemindedness

pure, steep, obsessive, touching, yes, heroic:
the voyage, driven, fixed, into the blossom.
How, then, in such matters, account for passion?
Deep in woods, late, too late, dusk falling, falling,
what shall one cry if not Down, Down, Come down?)

Somewhere south of here, tropical but vague,
a warmth, a heat, too dazzling to be conjured,
the sun begins its labor of ascension
at an angle precipitous, audacious,
through latitudes no doubt exotic, foreign,

hemispheres waiting to be named, uncharted,
expeditions yet to be undertaken,
where the lives others live must be imagined,
but too dimly, too poorly, in the end
(costly admission) unimaginable.

X, on a winter night I rose in darkness
so unambiguous, so unremitting,
the thing it cast so faceted, so final,
so many-sided, I could not distinguish
where pain, your pain, began, where darkness ended.

Seated at the foot of the bed, composed,
that composure beyond composure, gazing
not to left, not to right, calm, undistracted,
it moved, it spoke its name, it shaped a gesture,
a living sign—a beckoning? a welcome?—

unlike the sign pain elsewhere takes to shape;
it whispered Rise to follow, Rise to follow,
watching the way the dark scattered the words,
pure inundation, knowing, too, the sleep
the dream-struck sleeper sprawled before it slept.

I would have gone wherever it had asked,
even where it might never dare to ask,
touched, this late, by the words, need, invitation,
by the compelling gesture, small but vast.
I would have gone, have risen, traveled, followed.

I would have cleared a footpath, slashed a route
through the implicit chaos of the woods
(into, out of: need the distinctions matter?)
by which to grope our way against the dark,
a mere, dim progress, yes, but—look—a progress,

hacking at ice until earth's crust bled through,
parting the brambles, raging at the vines,
fashioning what one thinks of as a clearing
(how shall we name what must be named?), the process
intricate, slow, hard, long, never explained.

I dreamt the dream the bears dream cradling snow,
almost delicate, their curled forms, in sleep:
mullet and salmon, scaled in gold, triumphant
in the momentous push upstream, upstream,
flailing against the depths of blue, noon sky,

somewhere weather flawless, air perfumed, balmy,
slipping effortlessly across the shoulders,
a cloak to be donned against chill of nightfall,
propitious, X, the latitude, the signs,
even the least among them, the right signs,

cartographers poring over their charts,
lenses and quills at hand, The Book of Names,
holy text of a godless century,
propped before them, opened, fortuitously,
to the A's—thresholds, fresh starts, embarkations—

having, years ago, from candlelit studies
(flame guttering ceiling to vaulted ceiling),
arrived at April as a name just, fitting,
the choice neither prolonged nor troubled: April,
Hemisphere of Incessant Flowering.